Twenty to Make

Gift Makes

Search Press

First published in 2015

Search Press Limited
Wellwood, North Farm Road,
Tunbridge Wells, Kent TN2 3DR

Contains material from the following books in
the *Twenty to Make* series by Search Press:

Crocheted Purses by Anna Nikipirowicz, 2015
Sugar Brides & Grooms by Katrien van Zyl, 2015
Papercuts by Paper Panda, 2015
Fabulous Pompoms by Alistair Macdonald, 2014
Mini Cupcakes by Lorna Fleming, 2014
Washi Tape Cards by Sara Naumann, 2014
Easy Knitted Tea Cosies by Lee Ann Garrett, 2014
Leather Jewellery by Natalia Colman, 2015
Felt Brooches by Myra Hutton, 2014
Knitted Headbands by Monica Russel, 2011
Mini Mosaics by Aimee Harman, 2014
Faux Fur Fun by Alistair Macdonald, 2015
Sugar Christmas Decorations by Georgie
Godbold, 2014
Quilled Animals by Diane Boden, 2015
Modern Decoupage by Louise Crosbie, 2015
Modern Friendship Bracelets by Pam Leach, 2014
Tags & Toppers by Michelle Powell, 2008
Fabric Flowers by Kate Haxell, 2011
Crocheted Bears by Val Pierce, 2011
Knitted Wrist Warmers by Monica Russel, 2014

Text copyright © Anna Nikipirowicz,
Katrien van Zyl, Paper Panda, Alistair Macdonald,
Lorna Fleming, Sara Naumann, Lee Ann Garrett,
Natalia Colman, Myra Hutton, Monica Russel,
Aimee Harman, Georgie Godbold, Diane Boden,
Louise Crosbie, Pam Leach, Michelle Powell,
Kate Haxell, Val Pierce

Photographs by Debbie Patterson and
Paul Bricknell at Search Press Studios;
Fiona Murray and Simon Pask on location

Photographs and design copyright
© Search Press Ltd 2015

Print ISBN: 978-1-78221-303-1

The Publishers and authors can accept no
responsibility for any consequences arising from
the information, advice or instructions given in
this publication.

Suppliers
If you have difficulty in obtaining any of the
materials and equipment mentioned in this book,
then please visit the Search Press website for
details of suppliers: www.searchpress.com

Printed in China

Contents

Introduction

This book is the second *Twenty to Make* taster we have produced and includes twenty-one great projects taken from a selection of fabulous *Twenty To Make* titles that have already been published.

We have included projects from papercraft, crochet, knitting, sewing and stitching, decoupage, sugarcraft, jewellery-making and mosaic-making books, so that there is something for everyone to try. We hope that experimenting with these projects will inspire you to try out some of the *Twenty to Make* books that these projects have been taken from, when you have had some fun making these tasters!

These projects will appeal to beginners and more experienced crafters alike; from making a lovely pompom cupcake, a teacup mosaic and a stunning, stencil-cut washi tape card; to crocheting a pretty purse, knitting a sweet tea cosy, and trying your hand at papercutting a beautiful mermaid or floral bouquet. You could also make a fabulous leather cuff, bake delicious mini cupcakes, or stitch a gorgeous felt brooch. These exciting projects are sure to appeal to a wide range of crafters, and will make lovely gifts for family and friends alike.

Have fun and happy crafting!

Twenty to Make Taster Projects
taken from these fabulous titles

www.searchpress.com

Bouquet

Materials:

Tracing paper
Pencil
Ivory paper
Coloured paper
Adhesive dots

Tools:

Scalpel (barrel handle
  and spare blades)
Self-healing cutting mat
Container for
  blade disposal

Tip: Place coloured paper behind the veined leaves and the central petals, and use adhesive pads or dots to raise the papercut slightly from the backing.

Flowers are so versatile that this bouquet is perfect for a greeting card or picture frame.

For nineteen other unique Paper Panda papercuts, see **Twenty to Make Papercuts**.

Ava

Materials:

1 x 100g hand of worsted yarn (UK light aran) in turquoise, 219yd/200m

Fabric for lining (optional)

Stiff iron-on interfacing (optional)

Hook:

4mm (US G/6, UK 8) crochet hook

Notions:

1 x large snap fastener

Finished size:

Each hexagon measures approx. 4in (10cm) wide

Instructions:

Hexagons (make 8)

With 4mm (US G/6, UK 8) crochet hook make 5 ch, join with sl st to form a ring.

Round 1: 4 ch (counts as 1 dc (*UKtr*) and 1 ch), [1 dc (*UKtr*) in ring, 1 ch] eleven times, join with sl st to third ch of 4-ch at beg of round.

Round 2: 3 ch (counts as 1 dc (*UKtr*)), 2 dc (*UKtr*) in next 1-ch sp, 1 dc (*UKtr*) in next dc (*UKtr*), 2 ch, [1 dc (*UKtr*), in next dc (*UKtr*), 2 dc (*UKtr*) in next 1-ch sp, 1 dc (*UKtr*) in next dc (*UKtr*), ch 2] five times, join with sl st to top of beg 3-ch.

Round 3: 3 ch (counts as 1 dc (*UKtr*)), 1 dc (*UKtr*) in base of 3-ch, 1 dc (*UKtr*) in each of next 2 dc (*UKtr*), 2 dc (*UKtr*) in next dc (*UKtr*), 2 ch, [2 dc (*UKtr*) in next dc (*UKtr*), 1 dc (*UKtr*) in each of next 2 dc (*UKtr*), 2 dc (*UKtr*) in next dc (*UKtr*), ch 2] five times, join with sl st to top of beg 3-ch.

Fasten off yarn.

Making up

Press each hexagon gently with an iron and weave in all loose ends. Using the diagram (right) as a guide, join the hexagons together using sc (*UKdc*) on the right side of the work.

Hexagons A form the sides; join to one side of hexagons B and C. Join each A, B and C on one side to the centre hexagon. Join D to each B on one side. Cut approximately 7½ x 13in (19 x 33cm) of fabric and interfacing, leaving ¼in (5mm) for the seam allowance, cut to shape and sew to the inside of the purse.

Sew a snap fastener to the underside of hexagon D and in the middle of the two C hexagons to finish.

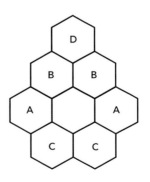

For details of other pretty purse projects and the yarns used to make them, see **Twenty to Make Crocheted Purses**.

Dancing Bride

Materials:

Modelling paste
  Flesh-coloured: 13g (½oz)
  Blue: pinhead-sized piece
  Yellow and brown mixture:
  5g (⅙oz)
  White: 63g (2¹/₁₀oz)
  Light blue: 6g (⅕oz)

Sugar/spaghetti sticks

Edible glue/pasteurised
  egg white

White and brown gel
  food colouring

Pink dusting powder

White lustre dust

Tools:

Cutting mat

Non-stick rolling pin

Scalpel/craft knife

Piping nozzle (tube)

Small paintbrush

Small blossom cutter

Toothpick

Dresden tool/skewer

Instructions:

1 Make a cone-shaped head, using blue paste for the eyes with a dab of white gel food colouring on the right.

2 Use white paste rolled into a large, thin cone to make the dress. Before making the pleats, roll the cone one third of the way up between your index fingers to make a mermaid tail. Pull a Dresden tool/skewer from the bottom of the dress towards the top to make pleats in the mermaid tail. Then pull it diagonally from the waist upwards in both directions to make pleats in the bodice. Push a long sugar stick or uncooked spaghetti through the cone so it protrudes at the top.

3 Make shoes from 3g (¹/₁₀oz) of white paste, rolled into ovals and attached to the bottom of the dress.

4 Roll out 3g (¹/₁₀oz) of light blue paste very thinly. Cut a long rectangle to go around the waist for a waistband. Cut out three small blossoms and attach them to the waistband with edible glue.

5 Make a neck from flesh-coloured paste rolled into a tapered sausage shape and attach to sugar/spaghetti sticks at the top of the dress.

6 Make arms and hands, then push sugar/spaghetti sticks into the top part of the arms to hold them straight.

Support the arms with cling wrap or small sponges so they dry in place.

7 Attach the dried head to the neck and turn it very slightly sideways.

8 Use the yellow and brown paste mixture to create an up style for the bride's hair.

9 For a satiny shimmer finish, dust the dress with a small amount of white lustre dust using a paintbrush.

For more details of how to make the
components of the Dancing Bride
and others, see **Twenty to Make
Sugar Brides & Grooms**.

Mermaid

Materials:

Tracing paper

Pencil

Ivory paper

Iridescent paper and glue stick (optional)

Tools:

Scalpel (barrel handle and spare blades)

Self-healing cutting mat

Container for blade disposal

Tip: Placing some iridescent paper behind the tail will give the mermaid an extra sparkle.

Mount this mermaid on sea-green or blue card as a pretty bathroom decoration, or make a birthday card for your own little mermaid!

For nineteen other unique Paper Panda papercuts, see **Twenty to Make Papercuts**.

Crazy Cupcakes

Materials:

1 x 100g ball each of light brown and red yarn

Scrap of yarn in a bright colour

Small amounts of white and yellow felt

Tools:

Paper and pinking shears

Tailor's chalk

Size 25mm (1in) and 45mm (1¾in) pompom makers

Pins

Sewing needle

Glue gun

Card for templates

Instructions:

1 Enlarge the templates provided below by 200 per cent and transfer them to a piece of card. Cut out and set aside.

2 With red yarn, make up one 25mm (1in) pompom. This will form a cherry for the top of the cupcake. Using light brown yarn and a 45mm (1¾in) pompom maker, make a larger pompom. Trim and shape each one into a neat ball and set aside.

3 Lay the cupcake case template on to some yellow felt and mark out with chalk. With fabric scissors cut out the sides and base curve of the case. To create the serrated top of the case, carefully cut this top curve with pinking shears (shown by the zigzag red line on the template). Bring the short edges together, overlapping by

about 4mm (⅛in), and pin to hold. Hand sew with a running stitch to secure in place, and remove the pin.

4 Take a scrap of bright-coloured yarn and wrap it around the felt ring. Use the jagged tops as a guide. Leave two jagged points in between each line of yarn. Continue to wrap the yarn around the whole case until you reach the start. Tie both loose ends of yarn inside the case to secure. Trim the ends and rearrange evenly around the base of the case.

5 Cut out the icing shape using white felt. Sew the cherry to the middle to secure. Assemble the cupcake by glueing the brown pompom into the case, followed by the icing topper complete with cherry.

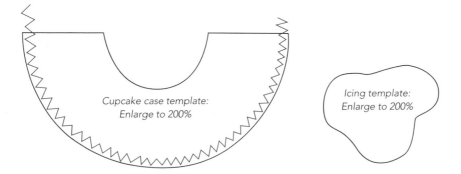

*Cupcake case template:
Enlarge to 200%*

*Icing template:
Enlarge to 200%*

For details of other fun and quirky pompom projects, see **Twenty to Make Fabulous Pompoms**

Mother's Day

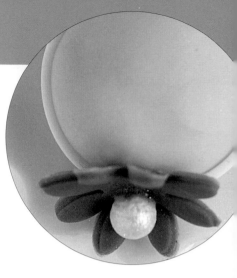

Materials:

Mini cupcakes

Buttercream

Purple, lilac and and peach fondant (sugarpaste)

Purple, lilac and peach flower paste

Edible glue

Nonpareils

Tools:

3.5cm (1⅜in) round, fluted cutter

Flower cutters, various sizes

Foam pad or greaseproof paper

Foam cupped drying tray

Craft knife

Instructions:

1 Start by making the flowers to decorate the hats. Roll out some flower paste on a non-stick work board to 1mm (¹⁄₁₆in) thick. Cut out several flowers in different sizes. It is best to have three tiny flowers to trim a hat, or one single larger flower. Place the flowers on a foam cupped drying tray to dry out. The tray shapes the petals, giving movement and dimension to the flowers.

2 The centre of the flowers can be made using a small ball of flower paste or, alternatively, a cluster of nonpareils. Either can be applied to the centre of the flowers using a small amount of edible glue.

3 To make the rims of the hats, roll out some fondant (sugarpaste) on a non-stick work board to about 2mm (⅛in) thick. Cut out fluted circles using the cutter. Set aside to dry on greaseproof paper or a foam pad.

4 Next, take some fondant (sugarpaste) and roll it into small balls with a diameter of roughly 1.5cm (½in). Place on a non-stick board and, using your index finger, slightly squash the ball into a half-sphere shape, so the underneath is flat. Make enough balls to top each of the fluted bases.

5 Apply a small amount of the glue to the centre of each base and then attach the squashed balls.

6 Next make the ribbon to trim each hat. Roll out some flower paste and, using a craft knife, carefully cut out strips of flower paste measuring roughly 3mm (⅛in) in width by 4cm (1½in) in length. The ribbon will be wrapped around the base of the squashed ball, so the length of the ribbon is dependant on the circumference of the ball.

7 Apply a small amount of edible glue to where the fluted base meets the squashed ball. Attach the ribbon and trim where necessary in order for the ends of the ribbon to overlap slightly.

8 Once the flowers have dried out, apply a small amount of glue to the back and decorate each hat around the rim (ideally covering up the join of the ribbon).

9 Set aside the hats to dry while you bake, cool and ice the mini cupcakes.

10 Apply the hats directly to the buttercream-topped mini cupcakes.

For the basic mini cupcake recipe and lots more decoration ideas, see **Twenty to Make Mini Cupcakes.**

Stencil-cut Flowers

Materials:

Washi tape: neon pink dot and stripe

Teal sheer ribbon

White, pink and cream cardstock

Pink ink spray

Blank white card 12.7 x 16cm (5 x 6¼in)

Foam mounting tape

Double-sided tape

Craft glue

Pencil

Tools:

Blossoms template

Circle punches: 2cm (¾in), 2¼cm (⁷/₈in), 5mm (¼in)

Detail scissors

Instructions:

1 Place five strips of washi tape on white cardstock, leaving a 4mm (¹/₈in) space between each one. Turn the paper over and trace a large flower from the template on the back, keeping your pencil on the inner edges of the stencil shape. Cut it out with detail scissors.

2 Trace the same flower on to white cardstock – this time, keep your pencil on the outer edges of the stencil shape to create a slightly larger flower. Cut out and glue the two shapes together.

3 Repeat to create medium and small flower shapes, placing the strips of washi tape slightly closer together.

4 Punch two 2cm (¾in) circles from leftover washi cardstock. Glue each one to a 2¼cm (⁷/₈in) white cardstock circle,

then use foam tape to attach to the centre of the large and medium flowers. Then punch a 5mm (¼in) circle of white cardstock and attach it to the centre of the smallest flower with foam tape.

5 Lightly spray cream cardstock with pink ink spray; when dry, cut to 11 x 16cm (4¼ x 6¼in) and mount the long edges on pink card using double-sided tape. Wrap twice with teal ribbon, securing the ends to the back. Tie another piece of sheer ribbon round the border and tie in a knot. Glue the piece to the card front.

6 Use foam tape to attach the three flowers to the front of the card.

Washi Embossed Flowers

Play with different surface techniques to give your blossoms even more dimension. Here I placed washi tape strips on to book paper, then stamped and heat-embossed an all-over design with gold. The combination lends texture and shine.

18

For more details on heat-embossing and other easy card-making techniques, see ***Twenty to Make Washi Tape Cards***.

Valentine's Day

Materials:

One ball each white and red worsted-weight (UK Aran) yarn

Tapestry needle

Two stitch holders

Polyester wadding

Needles:

One pair 4mm (UK 8, US 6) knitting needles

One pair of 4mm (UK 8, US 6) DPN

One pair 3.25mm (UK 10, US 3) DPN

Tension:

5 sts = 2.5cm (1in)

Instructions:

Make two.

Using red yarn and 4mm (UK 8, US 6) needles, cast on 42 sts.

Work 14 rows in SS.

Change to white yarn and continue in SS until cosy measures 15cm (6in) from the cast on edge.

Shape the top

Row 1: k7, k2tog, *k6, k2tog*, rep from * to * to last st, k1.

Row 2: purl.

Row 3: k6, k2tog, *k5, k2tog*, rep from * to * to last st, k1.

Row 4: purl.

Row 5: knit.

Row 6: purl.

Row 7: k4, yo, k2tog, k4, yo, k2tog, k4, yo, k2tog.

Row 8: purl.

Row 9: knit.

Row 10: purl.

Change to red and continue with SS for 14 rows.

Cast off.

Make up the cosy

Place the wrong sides of the cosy together (right sides facing out).

Sew the top

Thread tapestry needle with one of the white tails.

Sew 6cm (2½in) down one side, starting at the first white row.

Fasten off, hide tail in seam.

Repeat on other side of cosy.

Sew the bottom

Thread the tapestry needle with one of the red tails of yarn from the cast on edge.

Sew up one side for 4cm (1½in).

Fasten off, hide tail in seam.

Repeat on other side of cosy.

Make the hearts

For two hearts make four heart shapes.

Using red yarn and 3.25mm (UK 10, US 3) needles, cast on 3 sts.

Row 1: purl.

Row 2: k1, yo, k1, yo, k1.

Row 3: purl.

Row 4: k1, yo, k3, yo, k1.

Row 5: purl.

Row 6: k1, yo, k5, yo, k1.

Row 7: purl.

Row 8: k1, yo, k7, yo, k1.

Row 9: purl.

Row 10: k1, yo, k9, yo, k1.

Row 11: p5, p2tog, p6.

Work the top of the hearts following the directions below.

Do not cut yarn.

Make the first lobe

Row 1: k1, ssk, k1, k2tog.

Slip remaining 6 sts onto st holder.

Row 2: p1, p2tog, p1.

Row 3: knit.

Row 4: sl1 purlwise, p2tog, psso.

Cut yarn and pull through st.

Make the second lobe

Slip 6 sts from st holder onto needle.

Join yarn.

Row 1: k1, ssk, k1, k2tog.

Row 2: p1, p2tog, p1.

Row 3: knit.

Row 4: sl 1 purlwise, p2tog, psso.

Cut yarn and pull through st.

With tails and tapestry needle, sew two hearts together (right sides facing out) leaving a small opening at the top of the heart.

Lightly stuff hearts with wadding. Finish sewing.

Make the hanging cord

Using red yarn and the 4mm (UK 8, US 6) DPN, cast on 3 sts.

Row 1: k3; do not turn but slide sts to other end of needle.

Repeat this row until work measures approximately 25cm (10in).

Fasten off.

Weave cord through eyelets at the top of the cosy. Make sure both ends come out of the same eyelet opening.

Sew cord ends to hearts, pull cord tight and tie cord into a knot.

Love is in the air

What could be better than a steaming mug of tea to warm your heart and hands on Valentine's day?

For more beautiful tea cosy patterns, see **Twenty to Make Easy Knitted Tea Cosies**.

Painted Cuff

Materials:

3 x 20cm (1¼ x 7⁷/₈in) piece of vegetable tan leather

Leather glue

Small diamanté buckle

1m (39½in) length of silver suede cord

Silver fabric paint

1 x large snap fastener

2.5 x 19.5cm (1 x 7¾in) piece of nappa or pig suede leather

Tools:

Leather scissors

Rotary hole punch

Paintbrush

Cotton rag

Bone folder

Instructions:

1 Rub the edges of the piece of vegetable tan leather vigorously with a damp cotton rag. Then rub the edges with a bone folder until they feel smooth.

2 Paint the front and sides of the leather with silver fabric paint. The leather may need two or three coats of paint. Allow the paint to dry between coats.

3 Cut the leather cord into six equal lengths and thread them through the diamanté buckle. Apply a layer of glue along the back of the cords and stick them along the middle of the

leather lengthways. Trim any excess leather cord at the ends of the bracelet with the leather scissors.

4 Take the piece of nappa or pig suede leather and apply glue to the inside of the bracelet and stick the leather onto it, with the suede side facing outwards.

5 Once it has dried, punch a hole at each end of the bracelet and attach the snap fastener.

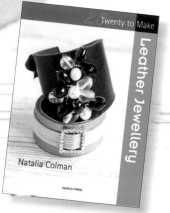

See **Twenty to Make Leather Jewellery**
for details on the technique used to make
the black cuff, and many more stylish and
desirable leather jewellery designs.

Chicken

Materials:

Tracing paper

Orange or light brown felt, 9 x 6cm (3½ x 2¼in)

Scraps of red and yellow felt

Scrap of red organza

Calico, 18 x 18cm (7 x 7in)

Wadding/batting, 9 x 6cm (3½ x 2¼in)

Backing felt, 18 x 18cm (7 x 7in)

Black thread

Brooch back

Tools:

16cm (6¼in) embroidery hoop

Sewing machine

Paper scissors

Fabric scissors

Embroidery scissors

Pins

Needle

Instructions:

1 Enlarge, trace and cut out the chicken template leaving a 1cm (½in) border. Trace and cut out the wing separately.

2 Stretch the calico on the hoop. Lay the wadding/batting centrally on top of the calico.

3 Lay the orange or light brown felt on top of the wadding/batting and the paper pattern on top of the felt. Pin across the centre through all layers.

4 Cut the red felt slightly bigger than the comb and the wattles, carefully slide these pieces in place under the pattern, tacking in place. Repeat with the yellow felt for the beak and legs. Pin all layers together around edges.

5 Using black thread and sewing through the pattern, start the outline at the top of the head, following the line over the curve of the head, then up and around the comb, along the line back over the curve of the head and body, and around the tail feathers. Continue along the outline to the right leg. Follow the outline of the right leg and foot, and stitch across the top of the leg before continuing along the outline under the body. Follow around the left leg as before and continue up to the beak. Sew around the wattles and across the top of the beak. Turn and travel down to the tip of the beak, then turn again for the underside of the beak. Follow the jagged feather line between the head and body.

6 Sew the inner tail feathers through the pattern in the same way as the head feathers.

7 Carefully tear away the tracing paper pattern.

8 Using the wing pattern, cut from a scrap of organza. Pin the wing in place and sew around the outline, creating feather shapes at the end.

9 Sew a few circular spots on the chicken's breast as shown.

10 For the eye, sew several stitches using a circular movement.

11 Carefully cut around the chicken outline, leaving a narrow margin.

12 Trim away excess wadding/batting and calico so that they sit just under the felt.

13 Place the work on the backing felt stretched in a hoop. Pin and stitch the outline. Start at the top of the head and follow all the way around the outline as before, turning sharply at corners, finishing at the starting point.

14 Trim away any excess felt.

15 Sew a brooch back onto the centre of the backing felt.

*Chicken and wing templates:
enlarge to 200%*

For details on felt brooch-making techniques and many other beautiful designs, see **Twenty to Make Felt Brooches**.

Versatile Mesh

Materials:

1 x 50g hank of 4-ply silk/merino yarn in variegated cream and purple, 225m/246yd

Needles:

1 pair 3.25mm (UK 10/US 3) single-pointed knitting needles

Instructions:

Using size 3.25mm (UK 10/US 3) needles, cast on 57 sts.

Row 1: k1, *yfrn, k2tog, rep from * to end.

Row 2: Purl.

Row 3: * sl1, k1, psso, yfrn, rep from * to last st, k1.

Row 4: Purl.

Repeat these 4 rows until work fits snugly when stretched around your head.

Cast off all sts.

Making up

With RS together, join seams together using mattress stitch. Weave in all loose ends.

*For more ideas on lovely headbands to knit, see **Twenty to Make Knitted Headbands**.*

Tea, Darling?

Materials:

Wooden teacup-shaped base

PVA glue

Pieces of pretty broken china

Pearl beads

Heart-shaped gem and flat-backed beads or gems

Glitter sand

Paint

Tools:

Tile nippers

Safety goggles

Paintbrush

Strong magnet

Plastic bag

Instructions:

1 Paint the wooden base of the teacup in a colour of your choice to hide the wood, as this project will not be grouted. Allow it to dry.

2 Using the tile nippers, start to cut up the broken china. This can be done safely within a plastic bag so all the pieces stay inside the bag. There will be some curved bits of china, if you are using bowls and cups, but by making them smaller, the curves lessen and the pieces will be flatter and easier to use as mosaic tiles.

3 Once you have a selection of flat pieces of china, you can start laying them on the board to see how they fit together. If you are using a heart-shaped gem, place it near the centre. Once you are happy that you have a good design, you can

fill in any gaps with little pearl or plastic beads, or any other embellishments you wish to use, to add some variety to the project.

4 Carefully remove the pieces of china you have laid out and try to keep them in order next to the base.

5 Using the paintbrush, apply some glue to the whole of the base. You can be generous with the glue, as it dries clear, so it is not a problem if it gets on the china.

6 Add the china pieces to the glued base, leaving some little spaces between the china for the glitter sand. Add the pearl beads and anything else you are using, and finish the handle with some flat-backed beads or gems.

7 Sprinkle the glitter sand over the whole project and gently tap it so it falls in all the gaps. Leave it to dry for an hour or so, then shake off the excess. If you do not want to add glitter sand, place the china pieces and beads closer together with fewer gaps.

8 Once it has dried, turn the design over and stick on a strong magnet with a generous dab of glue. Leave it to dry for at least an hour before using.

Note: This project can also be grouted as an alternative way of finishing the design, but it will not have a smooth finish as china tends to be rather bumpy and sharp.

For more beautiful mosaic projects,
*see **Twenty to Make Mini Mosaics**.*

Hot Water Bottle Cover

Materials:

Faux white tiger-printed
   rabbit fur

0.5m (19¾in) of lining fabric

5 x 100cm (2 x 39½in) of
   black satin ribbon

1.5 x 15cm (⅝in x 6in) of
   black grosgrain ribbon

One hot water bottle

Tools:

Fabric scissors

Scalpel

Thread

Sewing machine

Hand sewing needles

Chalk/pencil

Long, strong pins

Ruler and tape measure

Pattern paper

Iron

Instructions:

1 Make a pattern for your chosen hot water bottle. Lay out some pattern paper and draw round the bottle with a pencil. Remove the bottle and neaten the lines. Add a 2.5cm (1in) seam allowance round the whole shape. When you are adding the seam allowance round the narrow parts of the neckline, soften the curves as this will make is slightly looser, and therefore easier to remove the hot water bottle from the case. Make a second copy of this template and mark a horizontal line approximately 15cm (6in) down from the top of the bottle pattern. This will form the envelope opening to allow you to remove the bottle. Cut along this line. Add a further 3cm (1¼in) to both cut lines using additional pattern paper; these will form the overlap of the opening.

2 Lay all three pattern pieces onto the fabric side of the fur, paying attention to fur direction and any animal markings. Chalk round the templates and cut out using a scalpel. Cut out two bias strips of lining each 8cm (3¼in) wide and 30cm (11¾in) long. Press in half lengthways. Pin the folded edge of the bias along each straight edge of the fur (the envelope openings). As you are doing this, place 50cm (19¾in) of the satin ribbon in the middle of each piece (the length of the ribbon

should be running away from this edge). Machine stitch into place using a large stitch 5mm (¼in) away from the raw edge, combing the fur towards the centre as you stitch. To complete these sections, 'roll' the fur by folding the bias tape towards the fabric side of the fur and hand sew into position (see page 6).

3 Before assembling the main body of the case, hand sew the grosgrain ribbon to form a loop at the top. The loop should face away from the raw edge to be the right way round when turned through.

4 Now assemble the case. Pin the smaller flap to the bottle shape first and the overlap with the second flap. Match all of the edges and machine stitch closed using a large stitch, combing the fur as you stitch (see page 6) 5mm (¼in) away from the raw edge. Turn the case the right way out and insert the bottle to check fit. Fold the ribbon ends three times at 5mm (¼in) intervals and sew down to secure. Tie the ribbon in a bow.

For lots of fabulous faux fur projects, technique information and templates, see **Twenty to Make Faux Fur Fun**.

Christmas Pudding

Materials:

70g (2½oz) chocolate brown modelling paste

25g (⅞oz) flesh-coloured modelling paste

Small amounts of white, green and red flower/gum paste

Small amount of tan-coloured sugar paste

5cm (2in) polystyrene ball

One brown pipe cleaner

Cocktail stick

Red and green glitter

Pale pink dusting powder

Two white stamens

Tools:

Basic tools

Cutters: small and medium holly, large 6cm (2⅜in) blossom cutter, small 1.5cm (⅝in) round cutter

Clay gun or sieve

Fine black fibre-tip pen

Sugar glue

Instructions:

1 Roll out the chocolate brown paste, cover the polystyrene ball with a little sugar glue, then smooth the paste over the ball to make the basic body.

2 Using the large blossom cutter and white paste, cut out one large blossom and glue it on the top of the body.

3 Mark the pudding with indents using the rounded end of a pointed tool as shown opposite, then insert an 8cm (3¼in) cocktail stick through the middle of the body to the base for support. The top of the cocktail stick will support the head.

4 For the head, roll a 20g (⅔oz) ball of flesh-coloured paste into a smooth ball, use a pointed tool to make the holes for the eyes and nose, and make the mouth using the smiley tool. Insert two stamens for the eyes and mark the pupils using a fine black fibre-tip pen. Make a nose by rolling a small ball of paste into a round-ended cone, insert the pointed end into the hole and secure it in place using a little glue. Attach the head on to the body using a little glue.

5 For the ears, roll 1g (¹⁄₁₆oz) of flesh-coloured paste into a ball and cut it in half. Roll each piece into a ball then push the rounded end of a pointed tool into one of them. Add glue to the bottom part and place it on the side of the head firmly before removing the tool. Repeat for the other ear. When the head is dry, brush the cheeks with pale pink dust.

6 Cut two 7.5cm (3in) lengths from the pipe cleaner. Roll 12g (⁵⁄₁₂oz) of red paste into a ball and cut in half to make two ovals for the shoes.

Lightly glue both ends of a pipe cleaner, insert one end into a shoe and push the other end into the body. Repeat with the other leg.

7 Cut out two small red circles and glue them on to the base of the shoes to make little heels.

8 Cut the remains of the pipe cleaner in half to give you two more 7.5cm (3in) lengths. Roll 3g (⅛oz) of chocolate-coloured paste into a ball and cut it in half to make two round hands. Add a little sugar glue to each end of the pipe cleaner, attach a hand to one end and push the other end into the top of the body as shown. Repeat with the other hand.

9 Push the tan sugar paste through a clay gun or sieve to make spiky hair. Using a cocktail stick, lift a small section of hair at a time and glue the pieces in place, starting at the front of the head and working towards the back.

10 Cut out three medium and four small holly leaves from the green paste, then lightly glue one side of each and cover them with green glitter. Shake off the excess and leave to dry.

11 Using the red paste, make three small holly berries. Lightly cover them with glue and then glitter. Shake off the excess, then attach the holly and berries with a little glue to decorate the top of your little pudding's head and shoes.

*See **Twenty to Make Sugar Christmas Decorations** for a reindeer, Father Christmas, an angel, and many other lovely projects to make.*

Cat

Materials:

Quilling papers: 3mm (^{1}/$_8$in) strips in black, light grey, pale pink, and white; 2mm (^{1}/$_{16}$in) strips in light grey

Small piece of thin white card

Beige background card

Grey and pink chalk pastels

Tools:

Quilling tool

Small, sharp scissors

PVA glue

Ruler

Instructions:

1 Enlarge and trace the body and tail templates and cut out from the thin white card. If desired, colour the edges of the body and tail with grey chalk pastel as shown.

2 To make the ears, join a 5.5cm (2¼in) pale pink strip to a 5.5cm (2¼in) black strip. Roll from the pink end to make a coil, then pinch into a triangle.

3 For the eyes, make two pegs from 5.5cm (2¼in) black strips.

4 For the nose, make a coil from a 5.5cm (2¼in) pale pink strip and shape into a triangle.

5 Make two pegs from 5.5cm (2¼in) pale pink strips for the cheeks.

6 For the mouth, make a double thickness pale pink strip and trim to size.

7 For the whiskers, make a double thickness strip from 2mm (^{1}/$_{16}$in) light grey paper and fold in half. Glue another strip for the centre whisker and trim to size as shown.

8 To make the head markings, make three triangles from 5.5cm (2¼in) black strips.

9 For the body markings, make six triangles from 7.5cm (3in) black strips.

10 Make ten 4.5cm triangles from black strips for the tail markings.

11 To make the paws, make two semicircles from 22.5cm (8^7/$_8$in) white strips. Outline them a couple of times with black strips.

12 Make four 5.5cm (2¼in) teardrop shapes from 2mm (^{1}/$_{16}$in) light grey strips for the claws.

13 To assemble, glue all sections to the body and tail templates, except for the ears. Glue a black strip all round the body, beginning at the side of one paw, to define the shape. Glue another strip around the tail section. Then glue on the ears and tail. Shade the background card with the pink chalk pastel, then glue down the completed cat.

Cat and tail template: enlarge to 200%

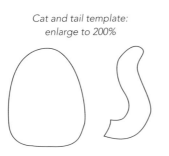

For useful quilling techniques and fantastic projects such as a mouse, a hippopotamus, a fox and a panda, see **Twenty to Make Quilled Animals**.

20 Twenty to Make

Quilled Animals

Diane Boden

SEARCH PRESS

Parisian Crackle Mirror

Materials:

1 x square-framed wooden mirror
Black and white patterned decoupage paper
Black or charcoal chalky finish paint
White chalky finish paint
Crackle medium
Decoupage glue

Tools:

Paintbrushes

Tip: If you cannot find any black and white patterned paper that you like, try making your own design with white tissue paper, rubber art stamps and some black ink.

Instructions:

1 Remove the mirror from the wooden frame and set it aside.

2 Paint the frame with a coat of black or charcoal paint and allow it to dry.

3 Apply a coat of crackle medium, making sure that you follow the manufacturer's instructions.

4 When the crackle medium is still slightly tacky and touch dry, apply a coat of white chalky finish paint.

5 Allow the paint to dry naturally and the cracks will appear.

6 Tear pieces from the decoupage paper and glue them to the frame. Because of the nature of decoupage tissue paper, it will blend into the frame and allow the crackle to show through.

7 Add a few more coats of decoupage glue, allowing each coat to dry before applying the next.

8 When the glue has dried, replace the mirror in the frame.

Learn useful decoupage techniques in **Twenty to Make Modern Decoupage** and transform household objects into fantastic pieces.

Festival Fun

Materials:

Designer: Laura Bajor

2 x large flat cord ends, 7 x 25mm (¼ x 1in)

5 x 6mm silver jump rings

1 x 10mm lobster clasp

2 x 12cm (5in) lengths of 20mm Liberty print cotton ribbon

1 x 12cm (5in) length of flat plaited (braided) white cord

1 x 12cm (5in) length of 4mm silver-plated cup chain

18 x 6mm dark blue pearls

30cm (12in) of 0.5mm waxed cotton cord

30cm (12in) of 2.5mm red suede cord

Tools:

Scissors

Flat nose pliers

Snipe nose pliers

Clear contact glue

Instructions:

1 Thread the pearls on to the 0.5mm waxed cotton cord, knotting in between each pearl. Leave 4cm (1½in) of cord at each end.

2 Fold the red suede cord in half and knot it around the cup chain, weaving it around the crystals to create a wrapped effect. Secure the suede cord to each end of the cup chain with a small dab of glue. Trim the ends of the suede.

3 Now take the two lengths of ribbon and fold and press them in half lengthways.

4 Gather together the two fabric ribbons, the flat plaited (braided) cord, the cup chain and the strand of pearls, and arrange them in your preferred order. Align the ends and insert them into one of the cord ends. Secure them using glue. Allow to dry.

5 Take the other ends of all the strands and secure them into the other cord end – you may need to adjust the lengths of the strands depending on your wrist size. Remember you still have to attach the jump rings and lobster clasp so allow for these too.

6 Using pliers to open and close the jump rings, attach three jump rings to one cord end and two jump rings and the lobster clasp to the other end. You can adjust the size of your bracelet by using either more or less jump rings.

Random Strands

Vary the colours, and use any left-over cords, ribbons and beads to make this pretty bracelet

For more information on knotting and plaiting techniques, plus lots more projects ideas, see **Twenty to Make Modern Friendship Bracelets***.*

Heart-felt Sentiments

Materials:
Coloured card
Organza ribbon
Glitter
Self-adhesive gemstones

Tools:
Scalloped square punch
Hole punch
Die-cutting machine and
  embossing folder
Glue pen
3D foam pads

For templates and lots of lovely
project ideas, see **Twenty to Make
Tags & Toppers**.

Variation
*Stick an embossed and glittered
heart on a rectangular mount. Mat
on mirror card and add to the front
of a greetings card.*

Instructions:

1 Cut the heart shape from coloured card using the template opposite, or simply make your own. Punch a hole in the centre of the heart.

2 Emboss the heart using an embossing folder in a die-cutting machine. Alternatively, use ready-embossed card or hand emboss using a stencil.

3 Outline the heart using a glue pen and sprinkle with glitter. Stick on two gemstones.

4 Punch a scalloped square shape and tie the ribbon around the square, threading both ends through the hole in the heart. Knot and trim the ribbon ends.

Patterned Daisy

Materials:

Card for template

Five pieces of lightweight cotton fabric, at least 14cm (5½in) square

Sewing thread

2cm (¾in) flat button

Decorative flower button

Delica or seed beads

3cm (1¼in) circle of felt

Finding as required

Tools:

Compasses

Paper scissors

Fabric marker

Fabric scissors

Iron

Hand-sewing needle

Tip
You need a fine, lightweight cotton for these flowers. If it is too thick, it will be impossible to gather the flower up tightly enough.

Instructions:

1 Using the compasses, draw a 14cm (5½in) diameter circle on the card. Cut this out to make a template. Use the template and fabric marker to draw a circle on each of the five pieces of fabric. Cut out the circles.

2 Fold each circle in half and press, then fold each into quarters and press again. Arrange the quarters in a circle in the order you want the petals to be.

3 Using the hand-sewing needle and doubled thread, work a line of running stitch along the curved edge of one folded circle. Pull the stitches up as tightly as possible to form a petal shape. Make a small securing stitch through the edge of the petal to hold the gathers in place.

4 Without cutting the thread, repeat step 3 with the next circle of fabric so that you have two petals strung together. Continue in this way until all five petals are gathered up together in a strip. Sew the two ends of the strip together to form the flower.

5 Make straight stitches across the hole in the centre of the flower and pull them up tightly to close the hole as much as possible. Make the stitches in every direction and pull them up evenly to keep the flower shape circular.

6 Stack the decorative button on top of the flat button and sew them to the centre of the flower. When making the last stitch through the buttons, bring the needle up through one hole, thread on three beads, then take the needle down through the other hole.

7 Add a suitable finding to the back of the flower.

Pink and Peachy

For a simpler look, make the same flower from a single fabric and use a large self-cover button, covered in the same fabric, for the centre.

From vintage to modern, there is a wide variety of beautiful flowers to make in **Twenty to Make Fabric Flowers**.

Mary Party Bear

Materials and equipment:

Crochet hook size 2.50mm (US B-1, UK 13)

No. 5 crochet cotton – 1 ball of ecru, 1 ball of red

Small amount of crochet cotton in very light beige

Brown floss for embroidering features

Short strip of red sequins

Small piece of marabou in bright red

String of approx. 50 small pearl beads

Toy stuffing

Sewing needle and threads in colours to match crochet cotton

Instructions:

Make the bear following the basic instructions at the beginning of the book, using ecru for the head, body, arms and legs and very light beige for the muzzle and ears.

Dress back

Row 1: Using red crochet cotton, make 21 ch, 1 sc (UK dc) in 2nd ch from hook, 1 sc (UK dc) in each ch to end, turn [20 sts].
Row 2: 1 ch, 1 sc (UK dc) in each sc (UK dc) to end, turn.
Row 3: rep row 2.
Row 4: sc (UK dc) 2 tog at each end of row [18 sts].
Row 5: sc (UK dc) to end.
Rows 6 and 7: rep rows 4 and 5 [16 sts].
Rows 8–10: sc (UK dc) to end.
Row 11: sl st across 3 sc (UK dc), work until 3 sc (UK dc) rem, turn.*
Work on these 10 sts for a further 8 rows. Fasten off.
Make frill along bottom edge of dress by working 2 dc (UK tr) in each st all along the starting chain. Fasten off.

Dress front

Work as dress back to *.
Continue on these sts for a further 4 rows.
Next row: work across 2 sc (UK dc), turn.
Continue on these 2 sts until strap matches back to shoulder. Fasten off.
Miss centre 6 sc (UK dc), join in yarn and complete to match other strap.
Work frill along bottom edge as for dress back.

To make up

Work the bear's features in brown floss. Sew the side seams of the dress. Take the sequin strip and measure enough to go all round the bottom of the dress. Stitch it in place along the last row of sc (UK dc), sewing through the centre of each sequin. Slip the dress on to the bear and sew the shoulder seams. Place the string of pearls around the bear's neck and tie it off firmly at the centre back of the neck. To make the head dress, wrap a piece of sequin strip around the bear's head, overlap it slightly at the back and stitch the two ends together. Take a tiny piece of marabou and stitch it to the join. Position the head dress on the bear's head and sew it in place with a few stitches. Cut a short length of the marabou to make a feather boa and drape it around the bear's neck.

Make Mary and a wonderful range of her cute and cuddly companions in **Twenty to Make** *Crocheted Bears*.

20 Twenty to Make

Val Pierce

Crocheted Bears

Sparkler

Materials:

1 x 100g skein of DK (8-ply) beaded yarn – turquoise; 250m/273yd

Needles:

1 pair of 4mm (UK 8/US 6) single-pointed knitting needles

1 pair of 3.5mm (UK 9 or 10/US 4) single-pointed knitting needles

Instructions:

Make two. Using 4mm (UK 8/US 6) needles, cast on 37 sts, then ktbl to form a neat edge.

Next row: k3 *MB, k5*, rep from * to * to last 4 sts, MB, k3.

MB: Make a bobble all in the same stitch. Knit into front, back and front again of same st, turn. Sl1, k1, psso, k1, pass previous st over. You are now back to the original 1 stitch.

Main pattern

Row 1 and every odd-numbered row (WS): Purl.

Row 2: *k10, sl1, k1, psso, yfwd*, rep from * to * to last st, k1.

Row 4: k9, sl1, k1, psso, yfwd, *k10, sl1, k1, psso, yfwd*, rep from * to * to last 2 sts, k2.

Row 6: *k8, (sl1, k1, psso, yfwd) twice*, rep from * to * to last st, k1.

Row 8: k7, (sl1, k1, psso, yfwd) twice, *k8, (sl1, k1, psso, yfwd) twice*, rep from * to * to last 2 sts, k2.

Row 10: *k6, (sl1, k1, psso, yfwd) three times*, rep from * to * to last st, k1.

Row 12: k5, (sl1, k1, psso, yfwd) three times, *k6, (sl1, k1, psso, yfwd) three times*, rep from * to * to last 2 sts, k2.

Row 14: *k4, (sl1, k1, psso, yfwd) four times*, rep from * to * to last st, k1.

Row 16: k1, *yfwd, k2tog, k10*, rep from * to * to end of row.

Row 18: k2, yfwd, k2tog, *k10, yfwd, k2tog*, rep from * to * to last 9 sts, k9.

Row 20: k1, *(yfwd, k2tog) twice, k8*, rep from * to * to end of row.

Row 22: k2, (yfwd, k2tog) twice, *k8, (yfwd, k2tog) twice*, rep from * to * to last 7 sts, k7.

Row 24: k1, *(yfwd, k2tog) three times, k6*, rep from * to * to end of row.

Row 26: k2, (yfwd, k2tog) three times, *k6 (yfwd, k2tog) three times*, rep from * to * to last 5 sts, k5.

Row 28: k1, *(yfwd, k2tog) four times, k4*, rep from * to * to end of row.

Repeat rows 1–17 once more.

Change to 3.5mm (UK 9 or 10/US 4) needles.

Next row: *k1, p1*, rep from * to * to last st, k1.

Next row: p1, *k1, p1*, rep from * to * to end of row.

Cast off all stitches.

Making up

Join the side seams using a tapestry needle and mattress stitch, 7cm (2¾in) from the wrist end (cast-on edge) and 5cm (2in) from the finger end. This will leave a gap for your thumb to go through.

Weave in all loose ends.

For many more stylish wrist warmer patterns in different styles, yarns and stitches, see **Twenty to Make Knitted Wrist Warmers**.

20 Twenty to Make

A fantastic craft series from Search Press

All *20 to Make* titles are available as ebooks. Please enquire at head office. UK tel: 01892 510850